W9-BGP-717

NOTHING IN NATURE IS PRIVATE

NOTHING IN NATURE IS PRIVATE

Claudia Rankine

The Cleveland Poetry Center
at Cleveland State University

CLEVELAND STATE POETRY SERIES XLIV

Grateful acknowledgment is made to the editors of the
following publications in which earlier versions of some
of these poems first appeared: *AGNI, The Black Scholar,
The Kenyon Review, Muleteeth, Pequod, River Styx,
The Southern Review, and Whiskey Island.*

Epigraph from *Notebook of a Return to a Native Land*
in THE COLLECTED POETRY
by Aimé Césaire
Translated by Clayton Eshleman and Annette Smith
University of California Press, 1983.

Thanks to Caroline Baumann, Sarah Blake, Gabrielle Glancy,
Mike Goodman, Polly Gottesman, Christine Hume, James Just,
Ann Scott Knight, Cliff Leaf, Peter Muz, Anne O'Connor, Beth Pray,
Maggie Winslow, David Wolf, Mark Wunderlich and Linda Voris.
Thanks, too, to Nuala Archer.

To Allison Coudert, Gordon Weiner, and
my parents, my deepest gratitude.

NUALA M. ARCHER, Editor
Design & Typesetting by THADDEUS ROOT

⊛ ⬭ 66

ISBN   1-880834-09-X (paperback)
ISBN   1-880834-10-3 (cloth)

Library of Congress Catalog Card Number: 94-071681

Funded Through
Ohio Arts Council

727 East Main Street
Columbus, Ohio 43205-1796
(614) 466-2613

For Walter

CONTENTS

I would go to this land of mine and I would say to it:
"Embrace me without fear . . . And if all I can do is speak, it is
for you I shall speak."
And again I would say:
"My mouth shall be the mouth of those calamities that have no
mouth, my voice the freedom of those who break down in the
solitary confinement of despair."
And on the way I would say to myself:
"And more than anything, my body, as well as my soul beware of
assuming the sterile attitude of a spectator, for life is not a
spectacle, a sea of miseries is not a proscenium, a man screaming
is not a dancing bear . . ."

– Aimé Césaire

NOTHING IN NATURE IS PRIVATE

American Light

Cardinals land
on a branch, female and male.
The sky shivers
in puddles created of night rain.
Speckled particles dance
in a path of light, so it seems
it doesn't matter what's in the road.
Then the shadow of a black oak
leans forward like a wounded man.

The lit landscape conceives
a shadow, its face dark, wide-open,
its eyes bloodshot
from what had come before.

...

In the lit landscape, in its peeled
back places, making the space
uncomfortable, representing no fault
in the self is a shadow
of a gesture of wanting, coveting
the American light.

A shadow on ships, in fields
for years, for centuries even, in heat
colored by strokes of red, against
the blue-white light—and in it
I realize I recognize myself.

...

And still the light
fills wind-tossed branches,
makes clouds iridescent
islands in the sky. And still
the same light (for nothing
in nature is private)
insists on a shadow in the road.

...

I step into my shadow
as if not to take it anymore,
and wonder where I am going.

Sweet sad shadow, sun charred
on the open road, I don't want
any trouble, don't wish
to be troubled, but when the sun
goes down on this aged,
dirt road, will I end
in dark woods, or make it home?

Birthright

Begin with white sheets
flapping amiably in the early breeze,
the heavens dawning biblical blue
and my mother teaching me to believe
in the goodness of mankind
but to trust no man.

Then, continue unfolding her story
until, naturally, it lives
to create shade around my heart.

Now, look at me. What I need to tell you
is this: When the only man I know,
my father, knocks, I'll lock him out.

...

At the dining room table,
picking chicken bits from a wishbone,
I hear my father's call. Once. Twice.

But nakedness is my identity
and fear, the red yes of my existence.

This was not what I asked for—
the man's face, which is my face, shut out.

everytime she sees a black man
she sees herself & can't separate
gender, & race

6

...

I dream I visit my own grave
but am not dead. I lie there uncovered,
my face, the image of my father's.
I turn away from my body, his.

...

Still, it seems he needs me,
and as my face turns away, my hand
reaches out. It can.

Why doesn't it?

Repeatedly, I ask my mother why
I feel naked in familiar places.

She wonders what I fear
that she does not already fear.

...

At home father plays solitaire
until all his cards face up.
At the bus stop mother and I wait.
A man jogs across the street
in the oily dusk. Grabbing my arm, she runs.

We pace in the falling darkness. The nakedness
of her, my own nakedness.

...

And again in the house, mother says,
Dear, look at you.
You've never looked worse.

Who she sees, the girl facing me
in the bathroom mirror, replies:

The way I look mirrors my father.
I am everywhere in the faces of black men.
Imagine the concern I feel for myself.

In Transit *— her mind and black people in society*

In the neighborhood, which is not
unfamiliar, which perpetually resumes
motion in the broadest daylight,

the complexion I'll know all my life
(the complexion of my fear)

is the secret that won't keep.

Around, out here, along the wide street
someone follows me. Stops when I stop.

Listens when I listen. I think,

Is this a game? And, of course, it's not.

I walk faster. My inhaled breath visible
in each glance locating my brother's jaw
in the killer's face. My blood spilling

and his body, a pulsing stick figure
to be shot down or etched into a cell wall.

...

Underneath a colored sky a man
wills himself to rise, each slow start
interrupted by police, their clubs

clubbing the man's head, his chest,
while the man, rather, the black man
(who is altogether a different thing)

is losing on the pavement. As a mother,
brother, sister, wife running red
lights past breathless asphalt, choked

buildings, I arrive again at the curb
squinting, craning forward, knowing
I've got to know: *Do I know this man?*

Do I recognize his body? Shattered
glass. Blue jeans. Hands up.
Face down. *Do I recognize him?*

10

...

Passing, what I heard
was the man asking,
the white man asking,
(as if he, the other
were going nowhere)
the white man asking
for a minute
of the other's time.

It seemed that he,
the white man,
had forgotten and locked
his keys in his car.

Simply that he,
the white man,
had forgotten
and was wondering,
if he, the other, could,
perhaps, get in, could,
somehow, please, break
in and get, please,
the keys out of the car.

...

moments of racial conflict

SHE:

Yesterday we made love on the floor,
our rhythm skinned my knee.
Today the insides of my thighs ache,
my knee burns, and love,
you have in mind, it seems, to come
and go as you please,
as if this country were a small town
you might grow old in.

HE:

Always I arrive to find you crying,
your tears taking anything
as their point of departure.

where is it that she can be safe

What can be imagined, you imagine.
Must I tell you again, I know better
than to go—or do—or be with—

SHE:

But, love, this is America and you
are what is human in my world.
Whenever I hear of another black
man dying, it's again clear.

...

I fold into my lover's body
His knee between my legs
His breath a metered presence in my ear

Then his voice, almost closed, so very quiet,
whispers, *Did I tell you, I was riding my bike
today on my way home from the gym, and a frat-
boy-type tried to cut me off with his car. When we
both stopped for the light—this was on West End
in the eighties—he yelled: "Hey nigger, why
don't you take your black ass back to Africa?"*

I fold into my lover's body
His knees between my legs
His breath a metered presence in my ear

[handwritten margin notes, left:] while people put him down (Rodney Kingesse)

[handwritten margin notes, right:] hears my world and hears what you need to understand about it

[handwritten margin notes, lower right:] can't escape it, a great love moment, then this blunt story and then back to love it's like they can't avoid it

...

There I was, watching the six o'clock news,
taking in juice and the sucking-in sound
of the helicopter in which commentators
hovered like flies, propellers going round
and round, disembodied voices yelling:
*This—can you believe it—this is live.
Live!* as the white man was beaten by
the blow-for-blow circle of black men

. . . arresting, but not paralyzing,
each blow demanded a look at the man,
at the men, then back at the man,

and the thing is, the time spent in front
of that screen was not as long as a minute
and the white man, pulled from his truck,
had done nothing, and still so much time
to understand, to feel the obvious held
up in the history trafficking my heart.

...

On our street,
no different from any ring,
living each minute
as his recovery
from being hit, he called
himself a boxer,
told himself: *Keep fighting.*

Until someone came to break it up.

...

Dining in an out-of-the-way cafe,
our wine glasses drained. A settled check.
And then midsummer, in its dusted light,
on the near-deserted street we, two
involved, arm in arm, between parked cars
and boarded-up warehouses. Car doors
opening. Boys emerged. Choreographed,
in agreement, our arms untwine. Him, me
slowly now in a sea of black youth, mouths
like small incisions: *Well. Well. What have*
we here, bourgie blacks in living color.
We two, closed in, but looking to the familiar
to mirror while speaking the slow *hello.*
And then one saying, *Let up. Let them go.*

...

Now whenever he approaches I turn to him,
put my hand to his heart. Sometimes I feel
nothing. What can I do? Where I want to go
is back into a childhood where my brother,
on his way out, walks past my room, looks in,
waves. But this is the present. Here, today,
a man walks down my street. Not a neighbor.
I do not know him. But I can see he is
a black man and so do not quicken my step
as I walk to my car. Where I want to go
is back into the house. Uneasiness makes me
uneasy as my hand, reaching the car door,
turns the key in the lock. Who I want to see
is my brother in the face of the man who was
walking and now stands close. He looks into
the watery vision of a woman he knows he does
not know. He wants and wants. What can I
give him? The kitchen knife he holds demands
everything. Sometimes I feel like nothing. Still,
I put a hand to his heart. He says, *Don't you
raise your hand at me. Don't raise a hand at me.*

[handwritten annotations: blackes with black lonly]

[handwritten annotation: don't hit me/fight back, she's just trying to say I'm your brother but he dosn't recognize her back.

recognize = relate/understand you]

17

...

The street makes the most noise and Maria is all motion,
words falling from her lips, her tongue sharp, feverish
when I tell her a kitchen knife was set against my cheek.

The man, Maria, who looked a lot like your cousin,
was forcing my arm . . . *Rubbish*, insists Maria,
if you need to worry, worry about white America.

Because of that America, violence seems kin to our skins.
On the hard, high stools we swing our legs like girls:
French fries, burgers, onion rings and Heinekens.

Mourning Song

The urge was to slice into myself—
to see my blood and know
who it came from—
how it got out into the world—

This was why I ran
the blade along my skin,
pressing its tip into what pulsed:

To make sense,
again, of the flood
giving way around me.

Doubling Back

Just to be able, within an hour's clarity,
to run and run the dirt path south,
in order to turn and run

the same path north—away from, toward
my life, every thought, like that—
lost within myself, the loss within

the life living in the doubling back—
the path I run away from, too soon
a path I turn toward,

and again on the street, sweat,
salt pooling on my collarbone, running
down my chest, along my spine,

into the waistband of my shorts,
onto the black tar, the grey cement,
sweat pouring out, sealing me in

to survive what is already lost.

Fragment of a Border

See me standing here
waiting for the light to change?
Recognize me. I
was born dark
with bloodshot eyes
and when the light turns,
I'll think, *Go.*

But there is no getting away
even if you will not see me.
In your face recognize

my Jamaican face,
an American face.

And if it only matters if
it's about you—
it's about you.

The Birth

What the red womb, torn
open, exposed, he enters
and finding no cradle, no
ready nipple, does not
think birth and feels
only strain, rawness where
nothing, no one should
have lived. He enters

and even here without
a name he finds his story,
older than the hills—
it is familiar, dirt
beneath his nails familiar.

...

And throughout, his cry,
forcing movement
of the Adam's apple in his throat,
echoes: For he would be
the sun risen, a tree
rooted, the cry in pleasure
released. For he would be—

except the seasons run cold.
The hot sun grows tired,
distant—an unwashed star,
a destroyed part. He enters
to find his will assumed broken,
to find his spirit swollen,
and the climate mean.

...

O glacial moon, O shadowed tide,
a man arrives
and the world asks him,
(as if he is the first)
what is your weight, the burden of you?

To which he replies: *If I as human*
am meant to live this way
then I will die or am dead
and some night in my decay,
this, my load, come down.

...

Overtaken sky. Disgorged rain.
Shivering. Spent. Always he was,
is here, is the land's bruised
utterance, stillborn in the back
of naked, stark—far from
a mountain top. What echoes across,
his cry—a shower of stones,
a tight rip, a hot loss.

And his birth, the taste of blood
in his mouth and freedom—
it is this truth (*O freedom*)
that binds him up (*yes freedom*)
ties him up (*dear freedom*).

...

In humanity—
into its strange house,
he enters—with will, more
brave than true, he enters
to find himself held in
by skin meant to restrain
the breaking heart.

And always the hurt
is all the same,
even if he wouldn't take it,
even if he wouldn't make it home.

New Windows

The stewardess gave me—I had just
turned six—a white eyelet sweater.
It was late November, 1968. "This is America,"
she told me, "cold, not like the West Indies.
One needs a jacket of some kind here."

I trailed off.

The white southern businessman needed
to talk. He wanted a story, or more
precisely, he wished to understand how
he came to be sitting next to me in first
class on that otherwise ordinary Thursday.

...

This morning when the doorbell rang
and a man stood outside my door,
I thought he must be official,
the doorman has sent him up unannounced.
So I opened my door to him,
smiled and said: *Good morning.*
He was a slender man in his forties,
blue eyes, with a part in his off-blond hair.
He kept both hands in his pants' pockets.
They were gray suit pants. For a minute
he said nothing, giving me time

to accept him as he looked past me
in search of—I'll use his words—
I need to speak to your employer,
to someone who lives here.

...

After he left—he had come
about new windows—I remembered
the southern businessman. His litany
of questions. His need to place.
The persistence with which he asked,
You aren't a lawyer, are you?
His curiosity had made me laugh,
so I told him everything,
described everything, including
the first airplane I ever flew in.
The one that brought me here.

...

It's been wanting to rain all morning
and without the sun subtracting
blue sky suggestions, it comes down easy
against leaves, sinking
in between blades of grass
as I enter to lower
wide-open windows
but find I'm leaning
forward, out, into this home.

Out of Many, One

Man called Country

Early morning him take
Windward Road to the beach,
drifting down far end

toward the fishermen
bent forward, them backbone
set against them flesh,

all of them muscle
gone tight
as the fish-filled net

is dragged from the sea.
Them two snapper, just there,
will do, Country say,

as him dimple pierce
him right cheek when him think,
already, though the day

barely start, them tired for true.

Back-a-Yard

Thirsty. Hot. The odor
of sweat at him nostrils,
Country harvest greens

from back field,
haul flats full of mud-caked
yams to the river

where water, blue
washed sky, run
brown along him arm.

Squinting against
glare, him speak to heat:
Lord it hot.

And rotting mangoes melt
yellow to brown
into roots of trees,

them sugar
soaking the earth,
calling flies

and him one goat
into the sun, a red tongue,
aflame in the sky.

Yard

From where she stand,
she see Country,
working them field

as she stir oxtail,
crushing dried herbs
between flat palms,

rubbing she hands clean
above the pot. Green spice
flake the bubbling.

All day hot steam rising.
Flesh pulling back from bone.
Red coals falling to ash.

Jubilee Market

Stalls along the road
sell merchandise in from Florida:
dungarees, Palmolive, root beer

and Cherry Coke.
And from a tape player set down
in a wagon of pineapples

Carnival's latest hit:
Agony.
Agony. Agony.

How him fret
as him walk side she
for him hear man say, *She,*

a beautiful woman.
Yes Mister. Desire
flattening out

on she floral print
back as hyacinths,
bougainvillea

cut on the bias,
are gathered away
from passing rain.

Into the gutter
water run to greater
wetness, salt.

The Interior

Naked as the day him born,
where mangrove trees
drop branches mid-trunk,

him ford Black River,
dreaming in words: *Me waan*
fi-me woman, me waan.

Red Hills Road

Crossing roots swell
like joints in earth
woven with vines

and chicory, and
sweating green leaf
press against leaf

on climbing stems
as Country drag him foot
on the path of red earth

leading to them ragged,
water-marked, wood
fence—him go enter

the house just now,
but him taking a minute,
for what him waan

say to she,
is him got to go: America.
Land full of opportunity

if you willing
to work. And him,
him willing.

36

Hellshire Beach

In atmosphere
turn blue with dusk
as cloud—

fronds tease
moon pieces
tossed to sea

sucking in debris
at water's edge
winds embrace them

with a grip
so rough
she turn and look toward it:

America go kill you,
but if you feel you must,
go 'long, go 'long.

Jamaica) men
leaving Jamaica to go
to America
women say you
get to do it

The Dark

Night John Crow glide
above them roof, crescent wings
reaching in black sky,

as the outside bear up
the latched door. Over him
long, slumbering body

she draw a sheet, tuck
him in with prayers, kneel
on the wooden floor.

West Harbour

Pansies, blue and white,
cover the green of she dress,
and she on harbour walk,

too far to hear, hear Country
foot drop as a throbbing
when him board the ship deck.

Him see she on the landing,
snapshot, blue mahoe tree.
Light of late afternoon

slipping from leaves
as him ship cut clean
lines through blue water.

At the ship's rear, the sea
heal itself. The sky
streak yellow and orange,

open into swelling dusk.

Him

West Indian, him left like de rest,
to sail for New York, to plant and pot
whatever fi root in de new soil,
dasheen, callaloo, fevergrass.
From somewhere him find chickens
for de rented backyard as him wait—
Lord, how him wait—for him Alien
Registration card. And when it come,
him toast himself: *Immigrant! American
immigrant!* So him talk and laugh
with him lips quick parting, *Who
feel dem can bad mouth America
don't know a damn thing!* But
soon him voice quiet (*Yes, Sir.*) Him
newness slipping clean into de past.
Holding two, sometime three job,
(steward, carpenter, cook) him give up
a few things (sleep, Red Stripe,
dominoes) for him waan believe, pursue,
dream de dream though something
put shadow pon him. (*Boy*) Glasses pon
de table. Head in him hand. Please.
Please. Him break him back, and for
what? (*Boy*) A promise no nothing.
So then, American women, nuff new
woman, him go through dem like
butter: Ackee and saltfish. Cassava.
Stuffed breadfruit. Oxtail . . . till
one Sunday him wake, and as sun full

him yard, him kneel ina grass and begin
weed him garden. Him little one see him
and ask, *What's his name?* And de
bigger child answer, *He's our father.*

Eden

A chicken thaws, blood
streaming in the sink,
circling dirty dishes.
Breasts and thighs slacken.
A chill lifts the wings.
Entrails bleed until
mechanically her hands
dress the white, pimpled flesh with
paprika, parsley. Then water
pours from the faucet,
splashing a hot, quick rhythm
against the rinsing dishes,
and she's returned to her own
water breaking and the first
child tearing through into
the marriage that drives her
from her world to this.

Once, the sun, a long blade,
divided what was home from now.
And she approached each day
with a large heart—the windwards
curling her flowered skirt
around her legs as she pulled
a chicken by its neck from inside
its wire coop—her mother,
in the hills, cutting cane with
a borrowed machete. Each feather
plucked from the fowl promised
a year of happiness with a man,
dark and handsome: *Sweet
surrender, gal. Sweet surrender.*

Barefoot, she remembers taking
the wash down to the river, running
almost. The others, her friends,
already there—their thick,
black braids pulled back,
their hands cooled by the water.
Pimples goose her arms
as a chill mounts beneath
her dress when the front door
opens. She looks up
accusingly at her children,
bags on their backs, knee-high
socks sagging at the ankles,
and behind them, at the tarred
street dusted by failing light.
Smoke roams the house, drifting
away from the oven, graying
the walls, the white curtains.

She

Daybreak, pon de continent she recall
how once she a farmer, a woman born
(St. Ann's Parish) in time (June 12, 1943)
with she gaze, brown-brown eyes,
favoring, perhaps, that of a dreamer,
though she surely been tried,
fi de English (dem ginnals) lived
in de hinterland, ruled pon de coast.
But lef that alone. Chickens ran yellow
flecks between de trees in them yard:
a mango, two coconuts, a guava.
And from de verandah—what she watched
since girl-time—de big belly sea.

Descending from Darkness

There is, by the way, an area
in which a man's feelings
are more rational than his mind . . .
—Ralph Ellison

On a bridge dismantled
half-way across the water
I am held

above black silence
deep
quiet in a night
pushing
its watery load south.

No barges.
A slated sky. Waves
sounding
a natural warning

as, again, I
reassure myself
I am breathing—

for more than death
can be feared—
I fear darkness,

its shadowy
presence,
like a thing's entire
weight, lowering

itself
into the *no*
resting on the soul
of this Negro.

My sense of myself includes
an organ for darkness
and the sharp, short breaths
of a woman opening
to breathe. Opening my mouth,

closing my mouth, as darkness,
like a low
exhausted wave, moves
through me
until this world is in me.

I lose hold of myself,
my place,
my exact presence.

Everywhere it is dark.

I try to see past
slaves—
who were a people.
They hand me a lineage of pain.
Do not say, *That was then. Those days*
were numbered. Avert your eyes.

If a child could cover
her face and conjure a home
where mother and father wave
contentedly from the yard—

I would.

But traced in my face
is what must be faced—mother
making her way to morning service,
her flat look, indelible,
saying—*Assault the air around me*
but take nothing else from me.

I am her, grown
and forever serious,
dark flesh
against the light,
an offspring, rigid—
bearing her pain.

I know a man who worked hard
at liking this life.
Shipped
to where the banks
are washed away,
the horizon gone,
my father's days opened
into darkness.

Enter the home
where I am raised
to live on and on
like this: a low-lying
weight, a shadowed
race. I am grieving.

My grief exists.

Excuse nothing. Judge nothing.
Question only how.

Say only: Once
there was this: slave ships,
lynchings.

Then I am injured.

My flesh welts,
discolors. My skin
burns through,
is marred
right through.

And what is least needed
is essential to life—

Darkness is the no, *no*
on my lips.

Colored by darkness, present,
lost, I put my hand
to my flesh and know

I am hurt.

        Never mind.

I open to close
above a river that trembles
a little—
whispering unsteadiness
in a world that will be narrow.

On this bridge dismantled
halfway across the water
I am held
or perhaps I hold myself—

for I will live
and I do live, and I
do not differ
in this land
which does not differ from the world.

I am slack water. I am uneasy motion.

                    I am beyond recognition.

Rest in my body
and know no
amount of living
will cure
the color on our race. Look
out of my eyes.

See the dark

and know
in this dark we are alone,

in this darkness we are more alone
than when we are alone

and what we are feeling,
how you are really feeling,

is drowned,

drowned, I know.

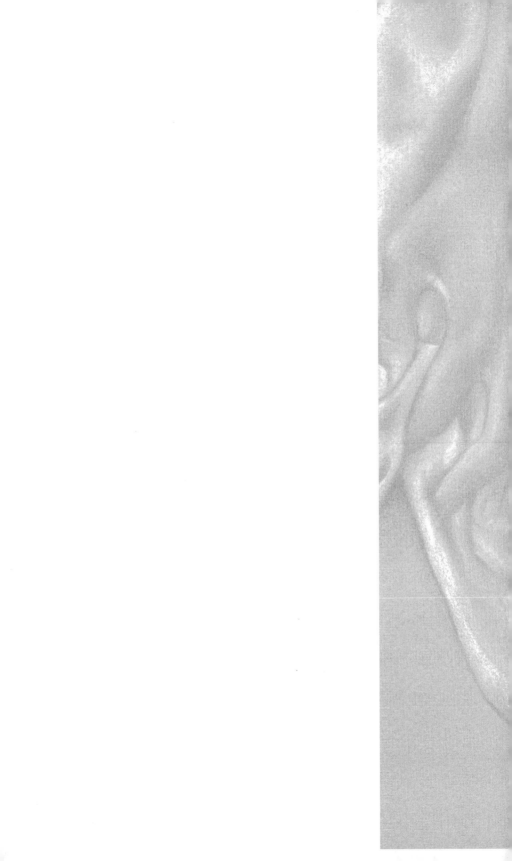

Refuge

In the field across the way,
Black Angus and rain.

Rain soaks low down
to the roots of the tall grass.

...

Or only yesterday I felt feverish,
as if existence were a sickness,
a burning away at—

I found myself in earth
of the lowest region, digging
with a will to surface,
to come up from years betrayed.

I found myself forcing a road
through destinies
walled and scarred.

Sweat soothes my brow.

...

And on the other side
are geese passing the night
on the Columbia River,
the brace of your weight,
the drooping cattails
and where the land was never
cleared, the forest of leaves
dripping into vermilion,
the wild geraniums.

The Man. His Bowl. His Raspberries.

The bowl he starts with
is too large. It will never be filled.

Nonetheless, in the cool dawn,
reaching underneath the leaf, he frees
each raspberry from its stem
and white nipples remain suspended.

He is being gentle, so does not think
I must be gentle as he doubles back
through the plants
seeking what he might have missed.

At breakfast she will be pleased
to eat the raspberries and put her pleasure
to his lips.

Placing his fingers beneath a leaf
for one he had not seen, he does not idle.
He feels for the raspberry. Securing, pulling
gently, taking, he gets what he needs.

Yearning for Children

The man, backing up onto wetter sand,
clutches a rod close to his chest.
His body is made rigid, his eyes fix
above the dunes on a red dot, a kite—
its invisible string unreeled all the way.

With the woman, as always, the sun
is stronger than she thinks—immediately,
she begins to darken; her talk, agitated
impatience, the fever beneath the skin.

She is seeing the man avoid the tide.
She is seeing his kite wire glisten

and then, again become invisible
as she runs into unridable waves.

On the Shore

The boy who holds the dazed butterfly
in his cupped hands does not differ
from the man, the same boy, but older,

who touches a lone finger to a pulsing
nerve in his neck: beating wing
slapping against his inner life.
He wants things settled without discomfort,
jarred movement, pain. What he desires
is what he's known: A country garden.
New moons. Full silences.
The land. The marriage that raised him.

...

Directly opposed to his need, a woman
pulls greasy potato chips
from a silvery bag, licks salt
from her fingers. She walks along
a lenient shore giving back
the in, the out, the rising
the falling off, the breath
of the ocean. Underfoot bits
of shell battered by time.

Who she is turns out to be the difference.

MoBay

October last year
a palmist said
a hand would break
the terrible fall
and rock me
through two seasons.

So consider the move
to the Caribbean,
how it takes me
completely, lures me
out-of-doors
where I give myself
walks in the water,
a new print dress,
lovers in MoBay.

And imagine
its sun: so red
and orange
and violet,
I wear it on my lips
as the new heat
blushes in me,
fills my cheeks,
brings the flowered
dress against my back
like second skin.

Sunset Returning

You! No you! He may be certain.
She may be right. Round and
round—each wanting the sunset:
the fiery, violent, but natural
end: spats of color, mixing black
and blue, jaundiced above, and where
light filters through, crimson.
Casual conversation taking
the turn for the worse. No doubt,
it's gone that way before. *Look!*
Listen! Closing her hand around
the emptied glass, she lifts it
absolutely to her mouth. *Damn.*
Pushing his chair back, he stands.
Nearing the horizon line: collide,
head on, go on—*love, oh love,*

oh careless—but then again no
one is laughing. Neither can
manage a smile. The phone rings
and rings. Both can hear it.
He refuses to pick up. She
draws a hand across her eyes.
And the sun, it sinks neatly,
dropping so far down, knowledge
of it depends on memory. What is
known, what is seen, what can
be done? It comes down to this:

it is clear, night resides here.
I love you, but—He holds
his face in his hands. She slouches
in her chair. And one does not
house more sadness than the other.

Plain Talk

The sky kneels close to the earth
like a voice becoming intimate
and turns him restless in their bed.
This is why he finds her, framed
by the doorway, ironing at midnight.
Following the iron back, forward, back,
he watches, hopeful—tomorrow what was
familiar will be familiar again—
though tears open into the blue fabric.
At their wedding she wore white;
the dress cascaded, its lace hem like leaves
against the floorboards. He remembers
holding her profile up to the future—her face,
the rich brown of mackerel beside his,
their promise settling earth into earth
in the unlit hills of marriage.
Now he feels like a man evolved
from the unnatural landscape of a dream,
and knows it is not that she doesn't, she does
seek within herself the way out, tries hard
to trim back their vows to this,
the only impossible life. Shaking his shirt out
she frees the heat against her body as if heat
could comfort on the worst of nights.
And hers is only one kind of existence:

sucking gently his lower lip,
he gathers himself close before turning
back to bed, trusting the ruby-throated
morning to provide her passageway.
For it's only her dreams that taunt her,
widening her eyes in darkness, blending
the untroubled night with her restless sorrow.
And how could he, forgiving her lack of ease,
collect her from her indigenous darkness
to lead her again to the resting world?
With what words could he summon her?
There is so little urgency in plain talk,
how could he simply say, *Sweetheart,
don't. Not to yourself. Not to me.*

How It Is

Walking the dirt road an entire hour early
to journey back to the mainland,

when the boy, generous with his concern,
wearing worry all over his face,
pointing to the sea, shouts, *Lady.*

Lady. Ship gone. Ship gone.

        She stares at him
unbelieving, as if, suddenly,
the ship,
out there, far from shore in full sail,
        is a phantom ship,

below an intense sun trying hard to focus.

Routine for an Insomniac

If anyone wants to know if you are all right,
tell them allergies, and that it's your worst
year, ever. Then take any bus to its last stop
before making your way to dinner where you
must soothe yourself with red and yellow peppers
in a tossed salad. Let the stripes of color
toned down by translucent slices of cucumber
make you the kind of woman who is disturbed
by bruised fruit. And just after you've eaten
let your insides separate: Two to one: Oil
to water. You know what I mean. Then listen
to yourself tell the taxi driver from Somalia,
after he's asked for your number, that you
believe in fate, and if, in the vast confusion
of downtown, he picks you up again, well . . .
Never be skilled at reckoning where your family
ends and the world begins. Be a product
of our ancient war: Let the enemy give life,
to advance until you tremble in the wind.
Then give up on Antigone—understand it is
useless to kill yourself over unburied corpses.
Instead, wonder if you are too late, for it is
already too late, always. At the toilet, bent
over, recognize you can never start a life here
receiving hard explosives for organs and a heart
with rust at its hinges. And finally, in the night
do not sleep running through the day
as if all life depended on your motion.

Landscape at Dawn

Darkness
grays
in the mist,

erasing hinted trees,
    weeds,
    wildflowers.

Then the path followed,
no longer there—Here exists

only you climbing up and up
and up through a moist wrap of air.

    Winded
        and exhausted,

you imagine this as the earth before
the heavens or trillium or you: this
as the earth in its solitude, inside
the solitude that rules the human being.

Within
you locate all defined parts of yourself,
    the lungs,
    the brain,
    the heart
    and so on,
to place on rocks like markers, to exist

regardless,

as you enter further this
body of mist, where each step taken

becomes all bruised time
        in the overdone spring,
another start toward a most dubious end.

Life, maybe, began like this:
        with the day,
        unyielding,
        unhewed,
rimmed with white walls of haze;

        with the flesh,
each of its organs vexed,
        unsteady
in the dammed air—certain
it won't take—can't have this!

        and with you,
who know most intimately
        this landscape,
feeling it disowns you

as you reach out in embrace
with no intent but to hold
as water rushes into pools

below.

Throughout

the dawn is yawning, is stretching,

is burning mist from shivering water

as you press on, decided,
for there will be nothing,

only this,
a body—only you

in motion upon the rocks, as life
takes up residence in this place.

Man and Woman in Landscape

Instead of emptiness,
a low moan
or the blue note of a swallow.

...

Conversation stops miles back
where the road ends before a tapestry
of seamless green and with eyes red,
chests heaving, they continue two,
maybe three hours across the English field.
When they speak it is of sheep
whose wool is heavy with dirt and rain.

My ambition, its full resolve,
goes with them past pink dog-roses,
fir trees. How hopeful I am.
After all I have seen, it is weak
to want them to love. Still
there are many things I want involving
that man and this woman in my body.

...

An old pain in a spring rain
and the same self with the red eyes.

I know how it is,
a body gets exhausted
but will not accept rest.

...

Either tears or a soft rain blur the landscape,
its purple-skin, blackberry vines, its wild
roses and the river they walk smack up against
with nothing left unfelt, all feeling joining
hands with the man and the woman who refuse
to put on raincoats and cannot be sheltered.

...

Everything,
all of nature,
rain wheeling
through dense trees,
everything
turns,
tears.

...

The air washes through, crisp
and clear and from the back steps, blue flats
are abandoned for a field of dandelions:
a million unvoiced wishes, yellowed
and multiplying.

Claudia Rankine, born in Kingston, Jamaica in 1963, was educated at Williams College and Columbia University. A recipient of the 1993 Kenyon Review Award for Literary Excellence in an Emerging Writer, she is presently a Visiting Assistant Professor of English at Case Western Reserve University in Cleveland, Ohio.

*The Cleveland
Poetry Center Press*
at CSU has been publishing
poetry since 1964. It is now
considered one of the outstanding
university presses in North America and
ranks as one of the top eight small presses,
specializing in poetry, in the U.S.
Located in downtown Cleveland,
The Cleveland Poetry Center
is also working to bring
these resources of excellence
to as wide and diverse an audience
as there are people in this urban,
lakeside, industrial setting.
Claudia Rankine's
Nothing In Nature Is Private
marks the 100th
book published by *The Cleveland Poetry Center*
as part of it's International Poetry Competition
which brings in over one thousand manuscripts annually.
Nothing In Nature Is Private
is the 1993 First Place
Winner.